M000211394

handing on the faith

Other *Handing on the Faith* titles:

When You Are a Confirmation Sponsor

When You Are a Godparent

When You Are a Grandparent

When You Are an RCIA Sponsor

When Your Adult Child Chooses a Different Path

Your Child's Baptism

Your Child's Confirmation

Your Child's First Communion

Your Child's First Penance

*"G*o into all the world and proclaim
the good news to the whole creation."
—MARK 16:15

_____

Catechist's Name

_____

Parish

_____

_____

When You Are a Catechist

Judith Dunlap

ST. ANTHONY MESSENGER PRESS

Cincinnati, Ohio

Nihil Obstat: Rev. Lawrence Landini, O.F.M.
　　　　　　　Rev. Richard L. Klug

Imprimi Potest: Rev. Fred Link, O.F.M.
　　　　　　　Provincial

Imprimatur: +Most Rev. Carl K. Moeddel
　　　　　　　Vicar General and Auxiliary Bishop
　　　　　　　Archdiocese of Cincinnati
　　　　　　　February 7, 2002

The *nihil obstat* and *imprimatur* are a declaration that a book is considered to be free from doctrinal or moral error. It is not implied that those who have granted the *nihil obstat* and *imprimatur* agree with the contents, opinions or statements expressed.

Cover and interior illustrations by Julie Lonneman
Cover and book design by Mary Alfieri

Library of Congress Cataloging-in-Publication Data

Dunlap, Judith.
　When you are a catechist / Judith Dunlap.
　　p. cm. — (Handing on the faith)
　ISBN 0-86716-483-2 (pbk.)
　1. Catechetics—Catholic Church. I. Title. II. Series.
　BX1968 .D855 2002
　268'.3—dc21

　　　　　　　　　　　　2002002027

ISBN 0-86716-483-2

Copyright ©2002, Judith Dunlap
All rights reserved.

Published by St. Anthony Messenger Press
www.AmericanCatholic.org
Printed in the U.S.A.

Contents

The Call to Share 1

The Gift of Faith 4

The Gift of Prayer and Ritual . . . 13

The Gift of Community 21

The Gift of Self 28

The Call
to Share

Thank you for saying "yes" to serving as a catechist—one of the most important ministries in the church. You join a long line of faithful Christians that stretches across continents and time, originating with the first disciples in Galilee. Just as surely as Jesus called each of them he has called you. By saying "yes" to that call, you open yourself to all the blessings that come with it.

Perhaps your initial "yes" was in response to a notice in the church bulletin or an appeal from the pulpit. Maybe you received a personal call from a member of the parish staff. Or perhaps being a catechist is part of your job as a Catholic schoolteacher. Whatever the circumstance or reason, whether you work with teens, toddlers, seven-year-olds or seventy-year-olds, your "yes" has set you on a path that can offer personal growth in both faith and knowledge as well as a great sense of satisfaction.

The word *catechesis* comes from a Greek word that means "to echo" or "hand down what has been received." A catechist is someone who hands on the faith. Being a catechist involves more than teaching religion—more than handing on the words and doctrine that define our faith. A catechist also endeavors to spark that intangible gift of faith that, accompanied by hope and love, marks us as Christians. Being a catechist involves heart learning as well as head learning.

The *General Directory for Catechesis* (*GDC*) tells us that there are six fundamental tasks of catechesis: promoting knowledge of the faith and moral formation, teaching others to pray and liturgical education, education for community life and missionary initiation. These six tasks are interdependent and develop together. Without any one of them the Christian faith cannot attain full development. We will look at each of these tasks in the pages that follow.

Handing on the faith might seem to be an awesome responsibility, but remember, when Jesus sent his disciples out, he made them a promise to be with them always. The same promise is made to you. You have already been blessed with many of the gifts you need, plus the assurance that whatever you ask for you will receive.

At baptism you were blessed with the gifts of the Spirit: wisdom, understanding, right judgment, courage, knowledge, reverence and an awesome awareness of the wonder of God. All of these gifts are available to you. In addition, other gifts come with being a Christian—gifts meant to be shared:

• The *gift of faith* received at baptism and recapped in the church's Creed.

• The *gift of prayer and ritual*, expressing a faith that goes beyond words.

- The *gift of community*, in which faith is nurtured, strengthened and challenged.

- The *gift of self* as a unique and precious member of God's family called to serve.

When You Are a Catechist will help you unwrap each of these gifts and discover different ways to share them in your ministry. After each chapter you will find some questions for reflection and discussion, as well as quotations from Scripture, the *Catechism of the Catholic Church* and the *General Directory for Catechesis*. Each of these books is important to our ministry. The Bible lays the foundation for our faith. The *Catechism* gives that faith shape. And the *Directory* offers reflections and principles to help guide us as we hand on that faith to others.

The Gift of Faith

*M*ary Ellen began teaching in her parish Catholic school when her oldest child entered kindergarten. *It was worth the cut in pay from her public school job just to be in the same building with her daughter. One of her concerns that first year was teaching religion. She considered herself a Catholic, but had spent very little time "practicing" her faith. She had been baptized as an infant and had gone to a Catholic grade school, but she did not remember much of what she had learned. How was she going to teach twenty-four eighth graders something she wasn't even sure of herself?*

As the year progressed, she became more comfortable trusting in the textbook her class was using. She soon discovered that she was learning as much as her students. Their questions became her questions, and in the process of staying one step ahead of them, she began to ask her own. By helping two dozen teenagers get to know God and their church better, Mary Ellen noticed her own relationship with God and the church growing closer.

That summer, Mary Ellen began working on her cat-

echist certification. She signed up for two classes on Scripture and the liturgical year. She chose both subjects not just as help for next year's class but because she wanted to learn more about the Bible and the church's seasons herself.

We all experience the gift of faith differently. For some it feels like a blazing fire touching every corner of their lives. For others, faith is like a tiny ember waiting for kindling and a gentle breath. How we experience our faith may change as our lives change, but for the baptized Christian, faith is always there. It is a gift from God, ready to be opened, waiting to set hearts on fire.

The job of the catechist is to invite others to look at their faith, and perhaps add a little kindling (even great blazes need to be fed). Often in this process the catechist's own faith begins to burn a little brighter.

So how do we feed the fire? We lay the kindling by teaching others about our Creed, our commandments and our sacred books. These words and stories have helped countless generations of people explain their faith. By handing them on, we offer others a way to express and find meaning in their own experiences.

Even more importantly, we feed the fire by helping the young people and adults with whom we work get to know and love God better. While we believe in the Creed, the commandments and Holy Scripture, ultimately our faith is rooted in Jesus Christ. Catechists promote knowledge in the faith so that others can not only grow in their relationship with Jesus but also act accordingly.

Promoting knowledge of the faith also means assisting in the moral formation of others. The old saying,

"Actions speak louder than words," is true. A person's faith is hollow if it does not affect how they act, the choices they make and who they are. The *General Directory* tells us that the definitive aim of catechesis is to put people "in communion and intimacy with Jesus Christ"[1] and to help them come to know "the paths that he has laid down for anyone who wishes to follow him"[2] (*GDC* #80).

Promoting Knowledge of the Faith

As catechists, we teach others about the faith, offering them a framework for their own experiences and giving them a language with which to share that faith with others. But most importantly, we teach the Creed, the commandments and Scripture so that others can come to know God and love God. No one is too young or too old to learn the words and stories that help explain their faith. Below are some ways of helping others to do this.

Look at the Big Picture. Before your first gathering, find out what you are responsible for teaching. Study the scope and sequence charts at the beginning of the book you are to use to help you understand how your teaching fits into the larger picture. It assures you that you do not have to teach everything. If there is no chart, ask your catechetical leader to give you an idea of the scope of your topics.

Set Objectives. Before each class or gathering, decide on what two or three ideas you want to be sure your students take with them. Write these ideas down in simple phrases.

Know Your Topic. Even when working with preschoolers there will be information you need to read and consider in preparation for your time together. If you need more information than what is provided in the books you are using, ask your catechetical leader.

Vary Methods and Techniques. It is important to vary your approaches. Use different teaching techniques during your time together. (See below for ideas.)

Check Out Resources. Videos, books, audiotapes, music and even people are all excellent resources. Check out equipment before using it. Make sure to view the whole video before showing it to others.

Know Who You Are Teaching. Faith is a very personal thing. It is unique to each individual. If you hope to reach the youngsters or adults with whom you minister, get to know them. Ask questions about their families, their hobbies and their interests. Find out what is happening in their lives. Adapt your teaching to their experiences.

Methods and Techniques

Attention spans vary, but few people can sit comfortably for long stretches of time. The younger the person, the shorter the attention span. With preschool or primary children, five minutes is long enough to listen to someone "teach." (Sometimes five minutes is long enough for adults, too.)

Try different approaches throughout the catechetical

process. Questions and answers, drawing, discussing or telling a story are only a few ways to invite people to focus on a topic. Use videos. Try role-playing or working in teams. Let folks young and old sit, stand and even move around. Introduce music and try working with crafts, even for teenagers and adults. Collages, puzzles, drawings and paper sculpting are all good ways to learn through activities.

Moral Formation

The goal of catechesis is not only to promote knowledge of the faith but also to touch people's hearts and lives, assisting in their moral formation. In other words, we want them to live what they learn. When the *General Directory* talks about moral formation, it is referring to gospel values. Morality is more than a set of rules we live by. It is an attitude of compassion and right living. It is walking in Jesus' footsteps and actively working to make our homes, parishes, neighborhoods and world a better place for everyone. Christian faith is a commitment to Jesus Christ, "to think like him, to judge like him" *(GDC* #53. Cf. *Catechesi Tradendai* [CT] 20b) and to live as Jesus lived. The following are a few ideas on how to help others live the faith you are teaching.

Teach through Example. Make sure your words and actions model what you are teaching. Keep your promises. Make every effort to be just and fair, kind and compassionate.

Set Guidelines. Ask participants to help you determine

group rules that are respectful to others and to property. Set guidelines for listening and confidentiality.

Share Your Feelings. Model honesty by admitting when you are feeling joy or surprise, frustration, tiredness or even anger.

Apply Lessons to Life. Make sure there is time at the close of each session to talk about the various ways participants can live out what was discussed. Help them draw conclusions that can be applied to their own lives.

Catechetical Process

There is a simple catechetical process that works well with people of all ages. If you work with a textbook, you will probably notice that each lesson follows this process or one very similar to it. By becoming familiar with the process, you will be able to add your own ideas, making your sessions even better.

Begin with the experience of the participants. Ask those involved to look at the topic from their own perspectives, within the framework of their lives. Next, present the topic from the church's perspective, based on Scripture, doctrine or tradition. Finally, apply the teaching to the participants' own setting as they explore ways to respond in their lives. Following this simple process and taking the time to plan, prepare and pray will help to make your efforts a success.

Importance of Prayer

Finally, even before you begin to plan or prepare, take time to pray. As we will see in the next chapter, prayer and ritual are also kindling that sets our hearts burning. Before each session, pray to be open to the wisdom and understanding that God wants to share with you. Throughout your session, be mindful of Christ's presence with you and in you. After each session, pray for each person in your group. And whenever possible, take time to sit in silence. Open your heart to the Holy Spirit, the gentle breath that ignites the kindling and sets our hearts on fire.

For Reflection and Discussion

- *How did you receive your "call" to be a catechist? Why did you say "yes"?*

- *If you could choose only one statement of faith that the youngsters or adults you teach would come to know, what would it be? How can you teach it?*

- *What does it mean to walk in Jesus' footsteps? How can you teach others to do this?*

- *What techniques have you found successful in helping others to learn more about their faith?*

- *How has being a catechist affected your own faith?*

Catechesis, must, therefore, lead to "the gradual grasping of the whole truth about the divine plan,"[25] by introducing the disciples of Jesus to a knowledge of Tradition and of Scripture, which is "*the sublime science of Christ.*"[26] *(General Directory for Catechesis #85)*

[25]Cf. DCG (1971) 24.

[26]DV 25a.

Then their eyes were opened, and they recognized him; and he vanished from their sight. They said to each other, "Were not our hearts burning within us while he was talking to us on the road, while he was opening the scriptures to us?" (Luke 24:31–32)

The believer has received faith from others and should hand it on to others. Our love for Jesus and for our neighbor impels us to speak to others about our faith. Each believer is thus a link in the great chain of believers. I cannot believe without being carried by the faith of others, and by my faith I help support others in the faith. *(Catechism of the Catholic Church #166)*

Notes in the Original

[1]*CT* 5; cf. *CCC* 426; *AG* 14a. In relation to this christological end of catechesis see part one, chap. I and part two, chap. I. "*Jesus Christ mediator and fullness of Revelation*" and that which is said in part two, chap. I "*Christianity of the evangelical mission.*"

[2]*CT* 20c.

The Gift of
Prayer and Ritual

*P*hyllis *was one of the best catechists I ever worked
with. She was genuinely interested in her students.
She knew them all and they knew her. She was an honest
and caring person. Prayer was important to Phyllis and
her class knew it. I remember the evening I discovered
this truth.*

*Phyllis was teaching twenty-six sixth-graders. We
were six weeks into the program when some parents came
to my office asking where their youngsters were. Class
had been over for ten minutes and Phyllis's class still
hadn't come out. I went to her classroom, cracked open
the door and was amazed at what I saw.*

*Twenty-six young people were sitting silently in a cir-
cle passing around a candle in the dark. I watched as a
young boy handed the light to another boy and listened
as he began a prayer. I closed the door quietly and told
the parents their children would be out shortly. When I
talked to Phyllis later, she told me they ended each class
with that ritual, praying for themselves, their friends and
families. That particular night they had a lot to pray for.*

The following year Phyllis started a Sunday night prayer group for junior high students. They began to meet twice a month. Almost all of her students came, and many of the youngsters from the year before returned. Today, twelve years later, there is a flourishing junior high program at the parish. Phyllis is the junior high youth minister, and the prayer group is still meeting.

Prayer and ritual are two fundamental ways of expressing our faith. Though limited and imperfect they are our ways of connecting with the mystery that is God. When shared, they help bring people together by offering comfort and support. Through common prayer and ritual our faith is nurtured, and the community is made stronger.

Prayer is spending time with God. (If you want to get to know someone it is important to spend time with that person.) There are all sorts of ways of praying. Words, actions, thoughts and even silence can be prayer. When we set a certain order to our words or actions and continue to repeat the prayer in the same way, prayer becomes ritual. We call our church's prescribed, public rituals liturgy.

I remember reading a book, years ago, about the importance of ritual and tradition in a family (*Ritual in Family Living: A Contemporary Study* by James H. S. Bossard and Eleanor S. Boll). After studying hundreds of families, the authors determined that rituals do four things. They are euphoric, making families feel good about themselves. They are adhesive, bringing family members closer. They are disciplinary, teaching there is a certain order in which things are done. And they are vitalizing, giving life to families. Rituals can accomplish the same thing for a group or even a church.

As Christians, we believe we are sons and daughters of a loving God and members of God's family, the church. We have our own prayers and rituals, and even our own liturgical year. As catechists, we hand on the faith when we share prayers and teach prayers, celebrate ritual and educate others concerning the church's ritual. There are different approaches to teaching others to pray and various ways to celebrate rituals in the liturgical framework of the church family.

Teaching Others to Pray

Prayer is our response to God, who is always reaching out in love to us. People respond in different ways. By introducing young people or elders to a variety of approaches, we can help them find a way that works for them. By teaching others there are all sorts of ways to pray, we are helping them grow in their relationship with God. Below are some suggestions on how you can teach others to pray.

Pray Together. Begin and end each session with a prayer. Choose a familiar prayer (Our Father, Glory Be), so that the words can become familiar, or pray in your own words.

Ask Others to Pray. Have individuals from the group lead prayer or pray in their own words. Make sure you let them know ahead of time so they can prepare.

Introduce Songs and Prayers from the Liturgy. Choose

a song or prayer from the Mass and say it together each time you meet. Try saying the Gloria or the Creed, for example, with older students or adults. Try a simple prayer response for younger children.

Talk about the Meaning of Familiar Prayers. Look at a familiar prayer, such as the Our Father, line by line. Invite others to say the prayer in their own words.

Introduce a Variety of Prayer Forms. Talk about traditional prayer forms, such as the rosary or Stations of the Cross, but also consider introducing journaling, prayer drawings or guided meditations. Listening to music or even dance can be a form of prayer.

Take Time to Be Quiet. In this age of constant noise and busyness it is important to learn to be still. It is often in the quiet moments that we hear God's voice.

For centuries the church has recognized three types of prayer: discursive, meditative and contemplative. Discursive prayer can be rote prayers (Our Father, Glory Be and so on) or prayers we say in our own words. Meditative prayer is reading (usually Scripture) and spending time thinking about and processing a passage. Contemplation is being quiet, no thoughts or words, just resting silently in God's presence. Each prayer type can be adapted in many ways, practiced alone or with others.

Promoting Liturgical Education

We are a church of rituals filled with signs and symbols. We celebrate our sacraments using words and gestures that are centuries old. We gather around a table as hundreds of thousands of people before us have gathered, standing and kneeling, saying or singing our Amen. Our rituals help to define us as a church. Learning about them and celebrating them are part of catechesis. Below are a few ways to help others appreciate the gift of ritual.

Establish Prayer Rituals. Begin and end each session with the same ritual. For example, you might place a Bible or candle on a special cloth. Say a prayer together or read from Scripture.

Worship Together. Attend Mass or a parish reconciliation service together. Try to arrange a special celebration for your group.

Celebrate the Liturgical Year. Celebrate the liturgical seasons by using the appropriate color cloths for your prayer table. Celebrate Advent, for example, by waiting and preparing for a Christmas party celebrated during the Christmas season.

Read the Sunday Readings. Read Sunday's Gospel with adults or older children. Introduce the Gospel's topic for Sunday to younger children.

Tour the Church. Talk about the various things you see around the church. Make sure you use the correct names for items and places. If you are uncertain, check with your priest or catechetical leader.

The Eucharist is the church's first and most important prayer. It is the source and summit of our Christian life. Many of the words and gestures from the liturgy go back to the earliest church. When we participate in this ritual, we join in communion with the whole community of saints, both living and dead.

Building Community

Sharing prayer and ritual is a wonderful way to bring people together. Shared prayer and ritual not only offer personal comfort, but also help people, no matter their ages, feel connected to each other. Being connected is an important part of being a Christian. We are all part of one body, one church, one Christ. As catechists, our job is not only to teach people to pray but to pray with them, to teach them about ritual and also to celebrate rituals with them. It is our way of handing on a faith that is lived and celebrated in community.

For Reflection and Discussion

- *What is your favorite way to pray? Who taught you how to pray in this way?*

- *Have you ever spent time in silent prayer? What was the experience like?*

- *Share a family ritual from your own family today or from the family in which you grew up.*

- *What do you remember about your own first communion and confirmation? What preparation went into receiving these sacraments?*

Liturgical formation, for example, must explain what the Christian liturgy is, and what the sacraments are. It must also however, offer an experience of the different kinds of celebration and it must make symbols, gestures, etc. known and loved. *(General Directory for Catechesis #87)*

First of all, then, I urge that supplications, prayers, intercessions, and thanksgivings be made for everyone.... This is right and acceptable in the sight of God our Savior, who desires everyone to be saved and to come to the knowledge of the truth. (1 Timothy 2:1, 3–4)

In his teaching, Jesus teaches his disciples to pray with a purified heart, with lively and persevering faith, with filial boldness. He calls them to vigilance and invites them to present their petitions to God in his name. *(Catechism of the Catholic Church #2621)*

The Gift of Community

Many years ago, my husband decided to take his sophomore religion class on a weekend retreat. I went along to cook and help chaperone. Unfortunately, I could not resist the urge to preach. I had just finished my second year of theology study, and I was going to save them all.

I told them what it meant to be a Christian, quoting Matthew about turning the other cheek and giving your cloak as well as your tunic (5:38–42). They were brutally honest in their response. They told me how totally unrealistic it was, how they would be taken advantage of and laughed at if they were to act that way at school. I closed my mouth for the rest of the weekend and kept to the kitchen.

That group of sophomores eventually formed the core for a parish youth group. We met twice a month planning and facilitating various social, liturgical and retreat activities for the parish teens. For two years we worked, played and prayed together. We became a small Christian community within the larger parish community. At the *end of their senior year we met to plan our final Mass together.*

While deciding on a Gospel, one of them discovered Matthew 5:38–42. As she read, neither she nor any of the others present seemed to remember our retreat experience. They listened as if they had never heard the reading before. The fact was that they were hearing it for the first time. It took two years of experiencing Christian community for them to understand Jesus' words. They chose that reading for their final celebration together because they said that was what being a Christian was all about. It was a great lesson to me about how we learn through the power of community.

We can teach people what faith, hope and love mean, but until they experience these virtues, we are only teaching words and definitions. The *General Directory* tells us that there are two ways of fulfilling the tasks of catechesis: by handing on the gospel message and by experiencing Christian life *(GDC* #87). If catechists can create an environment of trust and Christian fellowship, they are already helping others to learn and grow in their faith.

There are, unfortunately, many Christians who have forgotten or never experienced the faith in which they were baptized. As catechists, we do more than teach religion, we help others experience what we read in books on religion. We till the soil so that the seeds of faith and the Word of God can be nurtured and grow.

The parable of the sower that Jesus told his disciples so many years ago is true today (see Mark 4:3–8). God plants the seeds of faith, hope and love but the culture in which we live often makes it difficult for those seeds to take root and flourish. It isn't easy to believe in the mystery of God in a world that wants ready answers, to hope in the unseen when so much of what we see seems hopeless or to love unconditionally in a me-first world.

God plants the seeds, but the catechist can help till the soil by creating an environment of Christian community. We all need the support and encouragement offered by other Christians. It is easier to accept the Word of God and live the gospel when surrounded by a people who believe in the Word and the gospel. We learn from each other as we share our faith, giving and receiving the hope and love each of us and the world so desperately need.

To be a Christian is to be in community, working, praying, learning and serving with others. We learn by doing. As a community we are on a mission to serve our God by serving each other and the world around us. Part of the catechist's job is to teach others about the importance of community, to help them learn through the community's life and to initiate ways of extending the mission of that community to the world.

Educating for and through Community Life

When Jesus began to teach, he formed a community. He taught his disciples how to love and forgive, how to be inclusive and to watch out for each other's welfare. The disciples learned from each other and from Jesus' example. We can do the same in the classroom or catechetical setting. We can teach by helping those we gather form and experience Christian community.

Build Trust. Spend time each session (particularly at the beginning of the year) letting your students come to know you and each other. There are numerous resources available to facilitate this process for various age groups.

Establish a Christian Environment. Set up some guidelines for respecting others. Do not tolerate gossip or anyone laughing at or putting down another.

Enjoy Table Fellowship. Schedule a regular break time and occasionally have a treat to share. (Check this out with your catechetical leader.) Jesus did some of his best teaching while eating with others.

Recognize and Affirm Each Other. Celebrate successes and special occasions. Engage participants in conversation before and after each session and during breaks to discover what is happening in their lives. Bring others into the exchange.

Appreciate the Larger Community. Talk about what is happening at the parish. Invite parishioners to give brief talks about what they do for and with the church community.

Engage in Parish Activities. Discuss ways participants can become active in various parish ministries.

The *General Directory* tells us that catechesis is an apprenticeship (see *GDC* #56). It is learning to be a Christian by watching, listening and practicing with others who are also watching, listening and practicing. We are a community of apprentices with Jesus Christ as our Master Teacher.

Missionary Initiative

An essential part of Christian community life is mission—reaching out to others, proclaiming the gospel in our actions as well as in our words. Again, Jesus is our model. He preached the Beatitudes and spoke of an obligation to the poor and oppressed, but he also fed the hungry, championed the persecuted and ministered to all those in need. He taught his disciples to do the same. As a catechist, you can inspire generosity and selflessness in the people with whom you minister.

Highlight Parish Outreach. Make others aware of parish outreach activities. Suggest ways children and teens can help out or participate with their families.

Facilitate Group Projects. Check with the parish staff or outreach committee for any projects you can work on as a group. Even small children can draw get-well pictures for parish shut-ins.

Share Faith at Home. Find ways to carry home the faith learning begun in the group. When working with children, send home discussion starters for parents and children.

Discover Christian Witnesses. Search magazines and newspapers together for people who are living out the gospel message.

Discuss Role Models. Let others know about the heroes and heroines in our faith, people both living and dead who can be role models.

Faith is learned by living it. We know that faith is not just found in the Creed we say at Mass. It is a way of life that is learned by living and serving in community with others. It is handed on in playgrounds and classrooms, in kitchens and cathedrals. The words of our faith take on meaning through watching, listening, working and serving with other Christians who live the words. As individual Christians give of themselves, the community and the individual become stronger.

For Reflection and Discussion

- *Name a group or organization that you really felt a part of. What helped make you feel that you belonged?*

- *Who has made you feel welcomed in your parish? How did they do this?*

- *What aspects of today's culture make it difficult to live a Christian life? How can you provide an environment in your parish or catechetical setting to overcome these difficulties?*

- *What has being part of a parish community taught you about your faith?*

- *How can you, as a catechist, help others participate in your parish outreach activities?*

In virtue of its own dynamics, the faith demands to be known, celebrated, lived and translated into prayer. Catechesis must cultivate each of these dimensions. The faith, however, is lived out by the Christian community and proclaimed in mission; it is a shared and proclaimed faith. *(General Directory for Catechesis* #84)

"Listen! A sower went out to sow. And as he sowed, some seed fell on the path, and the birds came and ate it up. Other seed fell on rocky ground, where it did not have much soil, and it sprang up quickly, since it had no depth of soil. And when the sun rose, it was scorched; and since it had no root, it withered away. Other seed fell among thorns, and the thorns grew up and choked it, and it yielded no grain. Other seed fell into good soil and brought forth grain, growing up and increasing and yielding thirty and sixty and a hundredfold." (Mark 4:3–8)

While not being formally identified with them, catechesis is built on a certain number of elements of the Church's pastoral mission which have a catechetical aspect, that prepare for catechesis, or spring from it. They are [among others] experience of Christian living; celebration of the sacraments; integration into the ecclesial community; and apostolic and missionary witness.[9] *(Catechism of the Catholic Church* #6)

[9] *CT* 18.

The Gift
of Self

Many years ago, I had a miscarriage that left me in an emotional and physical depression. I felt alone and isolated. Confined to the house, I refused to speak to friends or even read the cards they sent me. Worst of all, I felt abandoned by God. I knew God loved me (hadn't I been told that for years?), but I could not feel that love. As I focused on God's absence, I grew more and more desolate.

Throughout those days, my friends took care of me. They took turns arranging meals and watching my children. They left flowers and chocolate chip cookies on my doorstep. They continued to write and phone, asking my husband to relay their concern and prayers. Finally, after two weeks, I was able to leave the house and go to Sunday Mass with my family.

I remember coming back from Communion, sitting in my pew and trying to pray. I watched each of the women who had ministered to me receive the Eucharist and smile at me as she returned to her seat. Suddenly I realized what the "Body of Christ" meant. I might not be able to *feel God's love, but I could certainly feel theirs. They were Christ to me. I could welcome their love, God's love, and allow it to heal me.*

With the help of my family and friends, I began to reclaim my life and God's love. I have learned many lessons through the years, but I will never forget those women or that Sunday morning. I learned more about the Eucharist and the Body of Christ at that liturgy than I had in sixteen years of Catholic education.

We profess and celebrate a faith that is alive. Books and lectures can pass on what we believe, but faith is handed on by people who live it. There is an old expression, "Faith is caught not taught." It is caught by being around people who witness the gospel and, consciously or unconsciously, give meaning to complex and mundane issues through their words and actions. The greatest gift you give to the youngsters, teens or adults you catechize is the gift of yourself—your time, your energy and your compassion—as you give living witness to the faith you teach.

Time is a premium. With the many demands of job and family life, extra free time is precious. They say you can tell what is important to people by observing how they spend this extra time. You choose to use yours helping others learn more about their faith.

As a catechist you spend time not only in the classroom (or some other catechetical setting) but also in preparing for each session. There is the immediate preparation of reading the necessary material, deciding how it will be presented and gathering supplies. There is also the time spent preparing in a broader sense. There are meetings to attend and workshops and classes to help you become a better catechist. This gift of your time is a testimony to how important your faith is to you and is in itself a witness of that faith to those around you.

The positive energy you bring to your classroom or catechetical session is also a gift. It is as inspiring as the teachings you offer. Your task is to share the gospel of Jesus Christ and to show others that it is indeed "good news." Your interest and enthusiasm for the subjects and topics you talk about can be contagious.

Take time before each session to let go of personal problems or concerns. Try to find some quiet space, if possible, and center yourself in prayer, put everything on hold until the end of your session. Take a few deep breaths and let the Spirit energize you. If you are still tired, frustrated or even angry, be honest with those you meet. By talking about how you feel, you can help others understand how to deal with their own uncomfortable moods. The gift of your positive energy and honest feelings are a witness to the faith you teach.

We know that it wasn't just Jesus' words that forever changed the lives of his disciples; it was who he was and who they were when they were with him. Jesus spent time getting to know the men and women who walked with him and they spent forever believing in him. He shared all that was his and they learned to share with each other. He forgave and they learned to forgive. He loved unconditionally and they learned to love unselfishly. He was patient, unbelievably patient, and he changed their hearts and minds and lives.

Teaching as Jesus Taught

Jesus taught with authority.
> Know the material and be prepared to teach.
> Remember you also need to continue to learn about the faith.

Jesus knew who he was teaching.
> Get to know the youngsters or adults with whom you are working. Use language and examples from their experience.

Jesus built community.
> Establish guidelines that will create an environment of respect and trust. Spend time together in fellowship. Talk, share stories and so on.

Jesus taught his disciples to pray and prayed with them.
> Pray and teach others to pray. Share an appreciation for the prayers of the community, particularly the sacraments.

Jesus lived his message.
> With the help of prayer and practice, try to model the faith, hope and love that are at the heart of all our teaching.

Jesus served others and taught others to serve.
> Encourage a sharing of ideas and resources. Offer opportunities to serve and work together in the parish and in the larger community.

Jesus was patient.
> Try not to be discouraged if your efforts seem less than successful. It takes time for seeds to grow.

Jesus trusted in the Holy Spirit.
> Remember you are not alone. You have the backing of your church and the promise of the Holy Spirit to give you whatever you need.

We are asked to teach as Jesus taught, patiently to mentor the young people and adults with whom we work. If they are to believe and live the faith we teach, they have to see that we believe and live it when we are with them. Joy, peace, patience, kindness and self-control are all fruits of the Holy Spirit (Galatians 5:25). Through prayer and practice, they are gifts we can claim, model and share with those we have been commissioned to catechize.

Finally, remember that catechesis is a lifelong process, and we are all apprentices. We all need to continue to learn about our faith. We need the support and encouragement of the Christian community and the help of prayer and ritual. We are all part of God's plan to build a better world through the hope and love we find in our faith in Jesus Christ. Thank you again for saying "yes" to God's call, for sharing your gifts and handing on the faith to others.

For Reflection and Discussion

- *Who are the people in your life who helped you grow in your relationship with God? How did they do this?*

- *What saint or famous person is a role model for you as a Christian? Why?*

- *Name someone in the parish who seems to really live his or her faith. What qualities does that person possess that you most admire?*

- *What special qualities or gifts do you have that help you as a catechist? How can you nurture these qualities?*

No methodology, no matter how well tested, can dispense with the person of the catechist in every phase of the catechetical process. The charism given to him by the Spirit, a solid spirituality and transparent witness of life, constitutes the soul of every method. Only his own human and Christian qualities guarantee a good use of texts and other work instruments. *(General Directory for Catechesis* #156)

For this reason I bow my knees before the Father...that Christ may dwell in your hearts through faith, as you are being rooted and grounded in love. I pray that you may have the power to comprehend, with all the saints, what is the breadth and length and height and depth, and to know the love of Christ that surpasses knowledge, so that you may be filled with all the fullness of God. Now to him who by the power at work within us is able to accomplish abundantly far more than all we can ask or imagine, to him be glory in the church and in Christ Jesus to all generations, forever and ever. Amen. (Ephesians 3:14, 17–21)

The first and last point of reference of this catechesis will always be Jesus Christ himself, who is "the way, and the truth, and the life."[24] It is by looking to him in faith that Christ's faithful can hope that he himself fulfills his promises in them, and that, by loving him with the same love he has loved them, they may perform works in keeping with their dignity. *(Catechism of the Catholic Church #1698)*

[24]Jn 14:6.